D1736841

WITCHES

by
Therese Ruth Revesz

A
cpi
Book

From

RAINTREE CHILDRENS BOOKS
Milwaukee • Toronto • Melbourne • London

Library of Congress Number: 77-10626

Art and Photo Credits

Cover illustration by Lynn Sweat
Photos on pages 7 and 11, Wide World Photos
Illustrations on pages 10, 16, 17, 21, 22, 30, 32, 38, 41, and 47, Sam Viviano
Photo on page 25, Culver Pictures
Photos on pages 26 and 36, The Granger Collection
Photos on pages 45 and 46, U.P.I.
All photo research for this book was provided by Roberta Guerette.
Every effort has been made to trace the ownership of all copyrighted material in
this book and to obtain permission for its use.

Library of Congress Cataloging in Publication Data

Revesz, Therese Ruth, 1943-
Witches.

SUMMARY: Briefly highlights the history of witchcraft from the
story of Circe and Medea, early Greek "witches," to Sybil Leek, a
modern-day witch.
1. Witchcraft—History—Juvenile literature. [1.
Witchcraft—History] I. Title.
BF1566.R44   133.4'09   77-10626
ISBN 0-8172-1034-2 lib. bdg.

Manufactured in the United States of America
ISBN 0-8172-1034-2

Contents

Chapter
1

An
Unusual
Student

Sybil Leek was 11 years old the first time she went to a regular school with other children. Sybil's principal and teachers thought she was a very unusual student. So did her classmates. No other student drew charts of the heavens on the bathroom floors. But, then, none of the others was like Sybil.

Sybil studied her star charts to predict the other girls' futures. She also claimed to have a special gift that helped her—"second sight." With it, Sybil said she saw things that were going to happen.

But Sybil found that having second sight wasn't always an advantage. Sometimes she "saw" things she didn't like. One day, Sybil says, she saw that her best friend Elise would die. A few months later, her vision came true.

Sybil constantly got herself in trouble at school. And the circumstances were always weird. One year, she was bored in her math class. Instead of falling asleep in class, Sybil simply imagined that she was in another place, the English class next door (she liked English). Eventually, Sybil says, she concentrated so hard that she was marked present in both classes!

It's not surprising that Sybil only stayed in school for three years. People didn't understand her strange talents. Actually, there's a very simple explanation. Sybil claims she was—and still is—a witch.

Despite some people's ideas about being a witch, Sybil doesn't think she's odd. There have been witches in her family for many centuries. As a very young child, Sybil learned witchcraft from her grandmother who was also a witch. The old woman would draw the signs of the zodiac on pastries she was icing. She carefully explained what each one meant and how the information could help Sybil "see" into the future. She also taught her young granddaughter how to use herbs and plants for healing.

Sybil Leek certainly isn't the kind of witch most people picture. She's not an old hag with a black hat. She doesn't stir up a batch of toads' eyes and butterfly wings in a big iron cauldron. And she doesn't ride a broomstick or have a pet black cat. But, as history reveals, there are *many* kinds of witches. Sybil Leek is only one.

Sybil Leek calls herself a "white magic" witch, because she claims to heal people and predict the future.

Chapter
2

The
Old Religion

Sybil Leek probably says, "I am a witch," the same way another person would say, "I am a Catholic" or "I am a Moslem." The witchcraft that has been passed down in her family began as a religion thousands of years ago. In fact, witches called it "the Old Religion."

The practice of witchcraft started when the world was very young and people first began to believe there were gods. These gods were super beings whose powers were greater than any human's. People thought it was important to worship them. Naturally, people also wanted to ask the gods for help. But only the wisest man or woman of the village was able to call upon the gods. This special talent became known as witchcraft.

In the early days of witchcraft there were no cities, as we know them. People still lived in small groups, or tribes. Each tribe had at least one witch. And people would come to the witch for help.

Like any other religion, witchcraft had its own set of beliefs, ceremonies, and holidays. The followers of the Old Religion believed in a supreme being—a god who had power over everything, including the other gods. Witches also worshipped the Mother-Goddess and the Father-God. The Mother-Goddess was the mother of all and the ruler of the moon and the night. The Father-God, the father of all, ruled the sun and the day. When witches prayed, they usually tried to communicate with these lesser gods instead of the supreme being.

Witches believed (and still believe) that an enormous amount of energy flows from the supreme being. By mentally "plugging in" to this power source, the witch, too, becomes powerful. It's similar to the way a machine gets elec-

A witch coven has 13 members. The thirteenth member is the high priest or priestess.

tricity from a wall outlet. Witches make this "connection" by using certain spells and chants.

Witches have always worshipped in small groups called *covens*. Today, covens normally have twelve members and one high priestess— thirteen people in all. Each coven meets once or twice a month under a new or full moon. These meetings are called *Esbats*. Before a witch may join a coven, she or he must go through an initiation ceremony. Sybil Leek was initiated when she was 19 years old. The ceremony took place on a high cliff. And it began the way all witches' rituals have begun for centuries. First, one of the members of the coven drew a nine-foot circle in the ground with a black knife, a witch's most important tool. The coven then chanted a prayer, asking that everyone inside the circle be protected from unfriendly forces.

When she was only 19 years old, Sybil Leek officially became a witch. Witchcraft had been in her family for many generations.

Sybil Leek was blindfolded and brought into the circle. A black knife was held to her heart. The leader of the coven, the high priest, explained to Sybil what being a witch would mean. Sybil swore an oath of loyalty to the coven.

Today, Sybil Leek earns a living from her witchcraft. She specializes in healing, astrology, and fortune-telling. All kinds of people come to her for advice, and many claim she helps them. Unfortunately, not all witches have been as helpful as Sybil Leek.

Just as there have always been real witches, there have been myths told about witches since ancient times. The next two stories deal with two most magical witches made up by the ancient Greeks.

Circe– A Mythical Witch

One of the first witches to find her way into written history was *Circe*. She was a beautiful young woman who supposedly lived in the time of ancient Greece, 1,000 years before the birth of Christ. She was the daughter of *Helios*, the sun god, and *Perse*, a sea nymph. Most people who met Circe for the first time thought she was just a lovely young woman. They weren't frightened of her until they got to know her better. By that time, it was usually too late!

Circe had magical powers and a mean temper, a frightening combination. When Circe found herself unhappily married, she simply killed her husband. For this crime she was sent to live on Aeaea, an island off the coast of Italy. Even though her dead husband's family wanted Circe to be hanged, they were afraid of her magical powers and her powerful parents.

Circe was lonely and bored living in Aeaea. To amuse herself, she invited sailors from passing ships to visit her island. Once they landed, Circe led them to her palace, where she offered them a great feast. For "dessert," Circe turned the men's bodies into animals. But their minds stayed the same. In time, Circe collected a large number of extremely intelligent—but very unhappy—pets to keep her company.

Circe continued her amusing little games for years, until she met *Odysseus*. He was the wise and powerful King of Ithaca, one of the ancient Greek city-states. Odysseus was on his way home from the Trojan War, when his ship was blown off course. His crew desperately needed fresh supplies of food and water. Circe's island appeared to be uninhabited, except for a lovely palace surrounded by trees.

When the ship landed on Aeaea, everything looked peaceful, but Odysseus wasn't taking any chances. He sent only half of his men ashore, under the command of *Eurylochus*, to investigate the beautiful palace. On the way the Greeks found themselves surrounded by lions, tigers, and wolves. They were frightened at first, but the animals were tame and friendly. (They were, of course, the men whom Circe had changed into animals.)

As they approached the palace, Odysseus' crew heard soft music and the sound of a girl singing. Suddenly, Circe appeared. She invited the men into the palace for some food. All of the Greek sailors accepted her invitation with pleasure—except Eurylochus. He didn't trust Circe, so he remained outside to watch.

Circe sat the men down to a wonderful banquet. She served them all kinds of delicacies and fine wines. But the feast was not everything it seemed. Little did the men know, Circe had added powerful magic drugs to their food and wine. When the sailors had eaten their fill, Circe went up to each one and touched him with her witch's wand. Magically, they were changed into pigs! She then herded them into pigsties and threw them some acorns.

Circe waved her wand. Right before her eyes,
the men became pigs.

When Eurylochus saw what happened, he
raced back to Odysseus. Hearing the news,
Odysseus immediately set out for Circe's palace.
On the way, he met a young man who intro-
duced himself as *Hermes*, messenger of the
gods. Hermes warned Odysseus that Circe was
dangerous. But Odysseus refused to leave his
men in Circe's pigsties. So, Hermes gave
Odysseus a magic herb that would protect him.

16

Circe was as delighted to see Odysseus as she had been to see his men. Naturally, she tried to "entertain" him, too. But this time, when it was time for dessert, it was Circe who was in for a surprise. She touched Odysseus with her wand and said, "Hence seek the sty and wallow with your friends." *Nothing happened!* Instead of turning into a pig, Odysseus drew his sword and sprang at Circe in a rage. The terrified Circe fell at Odysseus' feet and begged for mercy. Odysseus made the witch swear to

Odysseus raised his sword to slay Circe. Would she turn the pigs back into men?

change his men back into humans and to let them all leave Aeaea safely.

Even after Circe solemnly promised to return his crew, Odysseus hesitated. But, in the end, he *had* to trust her. After all, she was a witch, and he was only *human*. Odysseus knew —and Circe knew that he knew—the power was in her hands. If he killed her, his men would be pigs forever.

Chapter
4

Medea—
A Mythical
Witch

With all of her magic wine and powerful spells, Circe couldn't hold a candle to her niece, *Medea*. Medea was very much in love with *Jason*, King of Thessaly. And she used her powers to help Jason get whatever he wanted.

Medea even helped Jason steal the famous Golden Fleece from her own father, *Aetus*, King of Colchis. The Golden Fleece was her father's greatest treasure. By helping Jason, Medea cut herself off from her family and her country. In return, Jason swore that he would marry Medea and always be faithful to her.

When Jason and Medea returned to Thessaly with the Fleece, there was great rejoicing. But Jason's father, *Aeson*, was too old and sick to take part in the celebration. Jason asked Medea if she would use her magic arts to make his father young again.

On the night of the next full moon, Medea left the palace alone. She built an altar out of flat stones and lit a fire. Then she killed a sheep as a sacrifice for the gods. Medea walked around the altar three times. She dipped flaming branches into the sheep's blood and lay the branches on the altar.

Medea then called for Jason's father, Aeson. She put the old man into a deep sleep and lay him down upon a bed of herbs. While Aeson slept, Medea put a large iron pot over the fire and prepared a special potion. She used "stones from the east, sand from the ocean, the head and wings of an owl, and crushed tortoise shells." Before giving the potion to Aeson, Medea tested it on a dead tree. She stuck the tree into the potion. When she pulled it out again, the tree was green and full of new leaves.

Medea knew her potion was ready. So she cut Aeson's throat and let all of his blood run

Medea's magic potion and spell were now ready for the aged
Aeson. Would it make him young again?

out. Then she poured the potion into his mouth
and into the wound on his throat. As soon as she
was finished, Aeson's white hair became dark
again. When he awakened, he was 40 years
younger!

Medea and Jason lived happily together for
several years. They even had two children. One
day, Jason met *Creusa*, the Princess of Corinth,

21

Jason's new bride didn't know her robe had been poisoned by Medea's curse.

and fell in love with her. Forgetting all that Medea had done for him and the promises he had made to her, Jason divorced Medea and prepared to marry Creusa. Medea was very angry at Jason. In revenge, she prepared a poisoned robe and sent it to the bride as a wedding gift. Creusa put on the robe and died on her wedding night.

Then Medea killed her own children, set fire to the palace, and fled to the city of Athens. No one knows whether or not Jason died in the fire.

Were Circe and Medea real witches, or were they only myths? We do not know for sure. Once, even the city of Troy was thought to be a legend. But since the ruins of Troy have been found, we know it really was a city. So perhaps these witch stories are really true. Even if they're not, history tells us of many other witches in other times and places.

Chapter
5

The Burning Time

During the Middle Ages, in the mid-1300s, a terrible plague known as the Black Death swept through Europe. Millions of people were killed by the dread disease. It was also a time of famines and earthquakes. Many people thought that the Devil caused these horrible events. They believed the Devil had a huge "army" of witches to help him. It was the beginning of what followers of the Old Religion call "the burning time."

Witches, demons, and warlocks gather for the witches' sabbath.

In those days, many people believed that witches worshipped the Devil. After all, the Father-God of the witches had horns. Didn't the Devil, the most evil enemy of all, have horns? Whenever a person was accused of witchcraft, he or she was arrested and tortured until a confession was made. Even people who weren't witches confessed because they wanted to stop their torturers.

In a witch hunt, there was no such thing as "innocent until proven guilty." Anyone could accuse anyone else of witchcraft. Usually, the accused was burned at the stake. Witch hunting became a very profitable business. After a witch was executed, the church, the town government, and the accuser split up his or her property. That's why rich people were often targets.

One man who took advantage of witch hunting was Matthew Hopkins. In fact, if a prize had been awarded for the World's Greatest Witch Hunter, Matthew Hopkins certainly would have won it. He accused hundreds of people in England of being witches. *They were all convicted!*

Satan makes his claw mark on an apprentice sorcerer.

Hopkins grew very rich at his trade. Then someone—perhaps it was a *real* witch—decided to turn the tables and accuse Matthew Hopkins. In the end, he got a dose of his own medicine.

Oddly enough, the witch hunts did very little to stop the practice of witchcraft. Quite the contrary, a whole new kind of magic and witchcraft grew up during the Middle Ages. Unlike the so-called "white witches" (followers of the Old Religion), the new witches *really did* worship the Devil. These "black witches" believed that the Devil was more powerful than any other god. By praying to the Devil, they could have anything they wanted. This, the "black witches" thought, was worth the risk of being burned at the stake.

Chapter 6

Eleanor and the Witch of Eye

Eleanor Cobham was married to Humphrey, Duke of Gloucester. As the Lord High Protector of England, the Duke was the guardian of his young nephew, King Henry VI. If the King died, his uncle, Humphrey, would become King of England.

In 1441, Eleanor Cobham and four other people were accused of being witches. Their crime was plotting to destroy King Henry VI by witchcraft. Condemned with her were two priests, Canon Southwell and Father John Hun. A man by the name of Roger Bolingbroke was also involved. He was an astrologer and an *alchemist,* someone who could supposedly turn different metals into gold. The fifth person arrested in connection with the case was Margery Jourdain, known as the Witch of Eye. The Manor of Eye was near Westminster.

For years, Margery Jourdain had made her living selling potions and charms. In 1430, she had been arrested for witchcraft. But she had been let go without being punished for her crime. One of her customers at that time was Eleanor Cobham. Eleanor had come to the Witch of Eye for some love potions that she could use on the Duke of Gloucester. The potions must have worked. A short time later, Eleanor became the Duchess of Gloucester.

At her own trial 11 years later, Eleanor Cobham admitted she again went to the Witch of Eye after marrying the Duke. Eleanor said she had gone back to see the witch to discuss a new problem. She and the Duke had not had any children. She hoped that the Witch of Eye could help as she had done in the past.

Roger Bolingbroke, Canon Southwell, and Father Hun went with Eleanor on her second visit to the witch. Together, Bolingbroke and the Witch of Eye made a wax doll for Eleanor. Supposedly, it represented her unborn child.

The Witch of Eye prepared a wax doll to help Eleanor Cobham.

But Canon Southwell said a Mass over the doll and baptized it. At this point, Father Hun began to suspect that the doll was for the Duchess to cast a spell and kill young King Henry. Father Hun told his suspicions about the wax doll to the King's great uncle, the Cardinal of Winchester.

The Cardinal had long suspected that the Duke and Duchess might try to kill the young King. All he needed to hear was Father Hun's story. He immediately had Eleanor and the others arrested on charges of witchcraft and treason. But, when questioned under oath, Eleanor stuck to her story about only wanting a child. The court was sure she was lying, and the wax doll was some magical way to kill the King.

Eleanor Cobham admitted that she had asked Roger Bolingbroke to tell her fortune. There was surely nothing wrong with *that*, she said. She only wanted to know what was going to happen to her, and to what rank she would rise. Of course, everyone knew that the next step up for the Duchess of Gloucester was to become the Queen of England. But to become the Queen, her husband first had to be crowned King. And for this to happen, young King Henry would have to die.

Eleanor Cobham and her accomplices were all found guilty of black magic and treason. In the end they only denied the charge of treason and not the charges of witchcraft. Canon Southwell died in prison. Roger Bolingbroke was hanged and his head was placed on London

Eleanor Cobham's punishment was to walk throughout the streets of London carrying a lighted candle.

Bridge. Margery Jourdain was burnt at the stake. Only Father Hun was pardoned.

The Duchess of Gloucester suffered a different fate. She was forced to walk barefoot through the streets of London carrying a two-pound lighted candle. The people of London laughed and heaped garbage upon her. After her last walk, Eleanor was locked away in Peel Castle for the rest of her life. She was lucky at that! While prison didn't compare with being Queen of England, it was much better than being burned at the stake.

Chapter
7

La Voisin

In the France of Louis XIV, Catherine DeShayes, the Widow Montvoisin, was known as *La Voisin*—the witch.

La Voisin started out as a simple fortune-teller. But she soon discovered that people would pay more for results than for predictions. A countess didn't want to know *if* a handsome man would fall in love with her. She wanted a potion or charm to make sure he *did*. In the same way, a merchant who needed money might ask La Voisin when his wealthy relative would die. If her prediction indicated that natural death was not in the near future, La Voisin—for a price—would help him out. She might give him a poison, for example, to shorten the wait.

Her unusual line of work earned La Voisin an outstanding reputation throughout France. She was a special favorite at the royal court at Versailles. Here the noble but greedy lords and ladies schemed for power and riches. Some prayed in church for what they wanted. Others turned to black witchcraft. They worshipped the Devil and asked him to grant their every wish.

Worshippers of the Devil often held a *Black Mass*, a ceremony in which the Devil is summoned. But the nobles of Versailles needed someone who knew how to lead the Black Mass. They also needed the right "supplies"—bat's blood, black candles, wax images, and victims for sacrifices. Once again, La Voisin would be glad to help—for a price.

One of La Voisin's most famous clients at the court was Madame Athenais de Montespan, the King's favorite. Mme. de Montespan had come from a very poor family, but she now wanted wealth and power. As long as the King was in

Worshippers of the Devil prayed to his demons.

love with her, she had what she wanted. King Louis XIV showered her with money, jewelry, and estates. Anyone who needed a favor from the King would do the same. Mme. de Montespan was, for a time, the most powerful woman in the French court.

But Athenais wasn't taking any chances. She had arrived at her position with the King with La Voisin's help. For extra protection, she also prayed to the Devil. La Voisin sold Athenais all kinds of love potions and powders. Then, Athenais bribed one of the servants to add them to King Louis' food. These love potions were made from bat's blood, frog and wolf parts. It's no wonder King Louis suffered from upset stomachs and dizzy spells! Nevertheless, with the help of La Voisin's potions, not to mention a few wax dolls that looked like her rivals, Athenais remained "Number 1" in the King's eyes.

One day, however, the King suddenly fell in love with another very beautiful young woman. Athenais was really afraid she would lose her position in the court. She went to La Voisin for help. La Voisin, of course, had the perfect remedy. She soaked a gown belonging to the other woman in arsenic acid. When the victim wore the poisoned gown, her skin would develop painful sores. La Voisin would then send "healing" ointments to the victim. These were actually poisons. Needless to say, the King's new

girlfriend suddenly became violently ill. She died shortly after her 20th birthday.

Just about this time, the chief of the Paris police force arrested La Voisin. She was tortured and burned at the stake. Even though La Voisin insisted she was innocent, there was a lot of evidence against her. In her house the police not only found the poisons but also the black candles and the other tools used for witchcraft. Nearby, they dug up bodies of other sacrificed victims.

The King was angry when he found out about Athenais and her black magic. But because of their long friendship, he protected her. At first, he kept her in the court. But then he decided that *he* would be safer if Athenais went to live in a convent—for the rest of her life!

Athenais and the other members of the court summoned up evil spirits to gain wealth and position.

Chapter

8

Witch Hunting in America

During the burning years, hundreds of people throughout Europe were either burned at the stake or hanged. But the most famous witch hunt of all took place in 1692 in New England. It all began and—fortunately—ended in the Puritan town of Salem, Massachusetts. A group of teenage girls in Salem pretended they had been bewitched. They accused people from Salem and nearby communities of being witches. The girls said these "witches" had cast spells on them and tried to get them to sign the Devil's book.

People accused of being witches were tried
and sometimes put to death.

The leaders of Salem believed the girls and
arrested the people they named. Most of the
supposed witches were not tortured. But some
of them were afraid they would be and confessed
anyway. Many were tried for the crime of witchcraft and were convicted. Several were hanged.

The Governor of the Massachusetts colony
suddenly stopped the trials and arrests. It seems

41

the girls had gone so far as to accuse his own wife of being a witch. By that time, over 150 people were in jail waiting for trials or hanging. Nineteen women and two dogs were hanged. One man had been pressed to death under heavy weights because he would not plead either innocent or guilty.

Chapter

9

Witches Today

Witches have had a long and unusual history. Stories about witches have appeared throughout the ages in almost every part of the world.

There were some good witches. In fact, they were probably the first "doctors." They used their potions for healing the sick or they prayed over a very ill person, asking the gods to make their patients well.

Good witches also had special chants and dances to make the crops grow. They prepared potions that made people fall in love. And they kept their villages or tribes safe. But there were also bad witches, the ones who used their powers to hurt instead of heal. No one would want a witch as an enemy. Some witches used "the evil eye" on their victims. One glance from a bad witch could mean real trouble.

Good and bad witches still exist today. They are known as white witches (the followers of the Old Religion) or black witches (who worship the Devil). White witches are often suspicious of black witches because they sometimes attack and destroy white covens. Real-life black witches can be frightening. One of the best-known is Anton Szandor LaVey, the leader of a large coven known as the Church of Satan, in California. LaVey and his followers claim that he is a very powerful black magician. They call him "The Devil's Avenger."

LaVey claims that he can curse people, cure people, and even raise great storms. He seems most interested in cursing people. And it appears that he's quite good at it. People who

Anton Szandor LaVey claims to be a black magician. Some of his followers call him "The Devil's Avenger."

quarrel with LaVey sometimes have more than their share of "accidents" and bad luck.

LaVey is married and has children. His wife, Diane, is the High Priestess of the Church. A few years ago, his daughter, Zeena Galatea, seemed to have special powers. Whenever she neared an electric appliance, it would short circuit. Proud of his little girl's talents, LaVey decided to baptize Zeena in the name of Satan. The congregation of the Church of Satan held a special ritual for this. They ended the ritual with the words: "Hail Zeena, Hail Satan."

LaVey and his followers hold a black magic funeral for one of his former coven members.

Did witches ever really ride on broomsticks
next to evil black cats?

The real truth about witches is that we still know very little about them. Can they really "read" the future? Do their spells really work? Can they control the weather, heal the sick, make plants grow?

Most people believe witchcraft is only for show. They think a witch's power really comes from his or her mind. Some people may "sense" more than others about the unknown, about the future. Is this because they are witches, or do they have ESP?

The argument between those who believe in witches and those who don't will probably last forever. Meanwhile, we are left to explain the "magic powers" of people like Sybil Leek and the other "witches" throughout history. So far, we cannot.

How about you? Do you believe in witches?